exurbia

Durham Academy Arts and Literary Magazine

2017-2018

from the editors

Art is catharsis; the stroke of a brush or the flick of a pen carry immense emotional force. Weight is lifted off of shoulders as soon as thoughts are transferred to paper. They say that art imitates life, but so does its creation, because from the worst pain, the most beautiful work can be produced. This year's submissions were among the most profound and nuanced pieces we have received in our years at *Exurbia*. That's something this issue conveys extraordinarily well, with its rumination on love, grief, and exuberant demonstrations of joy. Putting this issue together has been a pleasure for the editors-in-chief, and we thank the Durham Academy Upper School community for opening up to us with their visions and voices, and for making *Exurbia* all that it is.

Your editors-in-chief,
Olivia Chilkoti
Austen Dellinger
Sean Rutledge

table of contents

I.
how we love

moth boy

Esme Longley '20

red becomes you.
you don't like chocolate,

or maybe you do,
but you never take any of mine.

see,
i'm not sweet, and you're not funny.
see,
you don't even know when to pause right,

don't know how to stretch your tongue and make words unslur, untangle the

us from flustered

and enunciate like little feet tapping across shiny floors, no you don't dance.

but it's okay. i don't either.

we sort of just sit together, you know. you arch your eyebrows,

i purse my lips.
sometimes i wish that we were very fat so we could sit in the same places but still have our skin touch while we regard something that wasn't put in front of us.

the trees by the recycled aluminium bleachers took away the silver spoon. or something.

today, we sat on the bleachers and i tanned my hairy legs while you talked about your depression. you wouldn't look at me, and the veins on your arm reverse embossed like the back of cream letters. green ink on multiracial arms,
i want to pour water on your

paper wingspan
and watch you smear and disintegrate like spiderwebs. i want to let my fingertips move to where they are tangential with the back of your hands,

maths boy. i'm sad for you.

since i cannot make it o.k.,
i fold up my camo jacket and

mimic your hand clutch with myself and close my eyes at the sun and your hair and everything else that goes unplanned and
i add and

subtract scenarios where we coexist and no one gets sad and

i can use a kneadable eraser to full in the crevices in the back of your hands where your nails eroded your bloody human body,

dear god, it makes me want to hurt something.

Grace Gordon '19

Love Poem

Anonymous

Love Poem
-for my best friend

I feel like a Friday

she told me once, beaming.

Or maybe,

she said,

I feel like an egg
--Crispy on the edges, but still soft on the inside,
and if you poked me

she laughed,

All the yolk would spill out.

and I thought to myself:
it would be golden.

and all the love poems,
they aren't for us.
and even if they were,
i'm sure
they wouldn't be enough. because

I'd choose you:

A Friday sunny side up,

over eternal summer
or a red, red rose
every time.

I'd choose you:

brimming,
swelling,
with goodness
and light.

Sam Grant '19

Buttercup buttershine

Esme Longley '20

i want to call you buttercup, buttershine, yellow daisy, sundress, sunshine in my hair as we spin with hands fastened together like a cloverchain daisychain, they can only rupture apart the dying stems of our arms and the dark roots of our fingers to separate us. even my brown skin turns yellow, i could pass for a tan white girl right now, dated auburn genes spur the image on until i want to be redder than fire, pink undertone keeping my breath even, keeping me less yellow. i want to mix up my own skin colour in acrylics and add gray but i'm scared of different hues. but i want a lot of things, like, to skin myself and see if a pilot g-2 07 gives my corrugated muscles more texture, if i could colour my inside brown in stabilo pens, drive plastic cars up and down the hills of my ribcage, i want to know the pathways of my arteries like i know my route home from school. i want air on my physical lungs, and to cut out the inside of my legs with safety scissors, so when i slip my skin back on, like a flapper dress, i will swim in it for a day or so before it fits.

yesterday, i drove myself to the supermarket and i wore my white shirt and pressed pink pants, and no one knew i was there. i watched mothers ignore their children put peanut butter jars into their trolleys and girls with makeup and girls with no makeup and boys with makeup and i didn't wait for you. but i did look for you. i explored every aisle and pushed row after row of the cans of baked beans, like maybe if i pushed back one more, i'd find my narnia, an escape from Aldi. i couldn't breathe when the cashier had to leave her station, i kept thinking she'd pick me up and stuff me into the confinement of the metal trolley and shove me out through the automatic doors that breathe like fish's gills and the last thing i'd see is her walmart-blue manufactured jacket. and i was paralysed and gripped my dandelion jacket until i could feel my nails rip through the soft, living fabric of my hands. see, i don't know what to do with myself. i keep playing dress-up in flower clothing made by child labourers in india, and i stay up until 3 thinking about their little hands and the fucking machines and the monotony of making something that will never matter to you. i want more for them and i want to care more than i do right now, and i want you to see my daisy dress and tell me that's enough and to stop stroking my petal hair and tell me what i'm meant to care about when everything is so important.

i want to call you buttercup, buttershine, yellow light, dandelion, but the speed of light is too slow to cover you all at once. we'll solve problems, i think. I'll go back to my roots. you'll grow towards the sky.

Sam Grant '19

Metamorphoses

Jack Anderson '19

We watch butterflies float for the very first time,
As their old lives they dismiss;
What a magnificent metamorphosis! This,
A change in unrestrained bliss.

We stay watching them for a moment and then,
To the river you retreat,
Where you tell me you think we should get in
To reprieve us from the heat.

The water is treach'rous as it swiftly runs,
And cold, in the shade of the trees;
And the rocks are slippery making me sure
We'd fall and scrape our knees.

But despite any danger I follow you down;
And taking off a shoe,
I consider all of the places I'd go,
For the promise of being with you.

As the butterfly does not fear his first flight,
Although it's new to him,
So I don't fear being with you
In a way I've never been.

If I now alleged we were just friends
I know I'd be remiss.
What a magnificent metamorphosis!
This, A change in unrestrained bliss.

Sam Grant '19

Never With You

Mac Hays '20

When you slept,
curled into a ball,
next to me,
       but not with me,
on the bus after patting the seat beside you vehemently and I could feel your body warmth radiating from your cheeks as you smiled in your sleep,
I thought this,
this is what love feels like.
The 18th time you sat next to me,
       but not with me,
in science class after I had been moved because I was being too noisy with my friends and you scribbled on my paper and laughed at me
       but not with me
when I drew the strings of my hoodie into a tiny hole over my face
I thought this,
this is what love sounds like.
When you smiled at me as you stood next to me
       but not with me
and gazed into my eyes
and I struggled to make eye contact because
You open your eyes
so,
so wide
as if your always in wonder
and like a cat's they reflect the light of the sun and it's blinding
and I thought this,
this is what love looks like.
You, you are so undeniably, indisputably, unrepentantly you that it causes me to act without my head and do stupid things to get your attention because I want to have that permanent blush, warm, blinding light face fixed on me just one,
just one more time.
You, You are instant gratification like corn syrup. I've got holes in my teeth and hollows in my guts because I didn't eat my greens or listen to my dentist and I've gotten addicted to you.
       But not with you.
           Never with you.

Sam Grant '19

for the next one who decides to love you

Raguell Couch '21

Over the phone, you told me that you didn't understand. So I'll start here: when you were gone, I wanted to be gone, too. I wanted to be wherever gone was with you, so that you wouldn't have had to go through all of it alone. But you decided to disappear, right into thin air, as if the rest of the world didn't exist, as if we were just another stepping stone. I didn't hear you leave that morning, so I didn't get the chance to watch you pack everything you came with into the backpack you've had since grade school. All you had was just enough--you were never the type that needed much, which made it even harder. Sometimes, when I think of you, it seems like you were never really here, a figment of my imagination, or a long-lasting dream.

But I remember your love for the little white hardly-there flowers we'd drive by on the way home, how you'd hold them in your water bottle so they'd stay alive until we got there. I remember yellow-red sunsets you'd sit outside for, just so you could replicate them on canvas. You'd sit there all night, even as the yellow-red fizzled out and melted into darkness, you'd light candles all around you so the painting would get completed. Even then, you'd never admit that you were simply scared of the dark, because it left too many unanswered questions, too many options to consider. The night before you left, it was one of those endless days, the sun's reign stretching out for much longer than it should. That was your favorite kind of day. I might've ruined them for you, but I can't think of them without thinking of you, and I don't know what that says about us. I didn't mean to make you cry; I know how you hate to, because you think it's weak and tears are unretractable, but you couldn't help it. It changed me, and I know it changed you--but I didn't know it was my fault. If I had known, well, it probably wouldn't have changed a damn thing. You were stubborn, stuck in your ways, and I had the audacity to say something. When you left, I wished you had woken me, instead of speeding off into the fog of the early morning, erasing your presence. When you got there, it took you a year to send me a postcard, and not even a good one--not the kind that said where you were, but a flimsy one with a pair of sandals on it, Wish You Were Here. That made me laugh for the first time in months. When I called you, I wanted to know if taking me with you had ever even crossed your mind, if you knew I would've been there for you, with you, had you told me. You'd always seemed worldlier than me, big headed but chock-full of experiences I'd only read about. We'd lay there on the grass, thin blankets resting underneath us, you telling me the stories of world-class journeys you'd had that would put me to sleep, dreaming of me being there beside you through every one. I didn't know until after it all that you lied. I learned it from your sister, who told me you hadn't even been out of the country save one trip across the border when you were three. You were good at storytelling, but then again, there was hardly a thing you weren't good at. I wish I could've said more, done more, so that you wouldn't have disappeared into thin air and pretended it was all a bad dream. I hate you for that--leaving, because I should've left too. You shouldn't have gotten to make a decision by yourself that affected both of us because that was selfish to do to someone that loves you. But I hate you for making me love you and in turn, making you love me, because if we hadn't, I wouldn't have had to wake up to the yellow tape and a mint green convertible, smoking, splashed with red because you were on your way back because you thought we could try again. Before the yellow tape, I thought about leaving, having you arrive to an empty house on the lake full of broken promises. But I'm also not you, which is good, but bad in a way, too. I saw your car, mint green with angry splashes of red, and my heart stopped. You sent me a photo the day before you were supposed to get here, and It arrived in my mail that morning. Your watch was glistening, even with a few pieces of grass hanging on, it looked beautiful in the light. The convertible still had a body in the driver's seat, a mistake on the police's part, leaving them there, but they weren't wearing a watch like that, their watch was dull, not sparkling in the light. When you were here, you'd run through the fields, dodging the prickly vines and trees, but somehow, you'd end up scraped anyways. You always liked to run, it was in your blood. You don't understand--at least that's what you said--so I'll make it simple, finally, because that's what you always struggled with. I can't make you into who I want you to be, so I dare you to live freely, to find someone you love as much as I love you. I dare you to search for them, to harbor such pain without them that you cannot bear to see them without falling back into such a spell. Show them your renditions of sunsets, run through beaches and fields and mountains, pick flowers of all kinds and never look back. Let them encompass you, destroy you and put you back together. For the next one who decides to love you, tell them simply of your love for endless days, especially if they've only ever liked the darkness.

Maggie Wittman '20

Grace Gordon '19

Austen Dellinger '18

What a weird heart...

Jeanne Jung '18

He made me a heart.
When you force in the battery,
it flashes and glows
and radiates red light - love.
I love it -
when it's turned off.
When the lights can't blind you
from its awkward shape.
Those uneven edges.
When you can see the hardware.
The resistors
and wires
and LEDs
and nails.
When it's turned off,
you can see where the love is.
Tucked under the tangled wires.
Melted into the metal that sticks out the back -
it's prickly, too.
It always gets me.

And everytime I see it
A chunk of dark green plastic and hard metal
I think
What a weird heart…
I love it.

Austen Dellinger '18

Anna West '19

Andria Shafer '21

25

II.
how we suffer

Finn May '20

1 2 3 4

Leah Granger '18

Count the seconds until it's over. Count. 1 2 3 4. What do you do when you're in pain? Do you ever curl up into a ball so tight you can fit into a baseball glove? Do you ever take a bath so long you get your fingers mixed up with those raisins and bite into them? Do you ever eat your fingers? Do you ever shake that bottle like a maraca? I hear there's rice inside do you ever eat it? Do you eat them all? Are you hungry? Do you ever dare to eat when you're in pain? Do you let it eat you? Does that feel good to you? What do you do when you're in pain? Do you ever sit at red lights hoping they never turn green because you are reassured by the color red? Is that sometimes not enough for you? Do you feel like you would do anything to break away the white noise? To breakaway the white men? To break. I once broke a glass bottle to wash away the pain. I tried to get as many pieces of it inside my body as I could. I counted them as they stuck to my throat 1 2 3 4. Rest, ice, compression, elevation. This is what my father tells me to do when I am in pain. Rest. Last night I slept for exactly 22 minutes but I was in my bed with my eyes closed for 12 hours he said I got a lot of rest. Ice. My heart freezes often enough but I turn the bathwater on cold I let it cover me I let myself turn purple I hate the color purple I do not think the color purple looks good on me. Compression. I give myself hugs sometimes I do it with poetry and ponytail holders I do it with my high-rise leggings I do with my oatmeal sometimes my dog gives me hugs other times I wrap myself in my blanket tight as I can. Elevation. If I were to die today do you think I would go to heaven does my father think that is that what he means by elevation how to cure pain go to heaven there is no pain in heaven. They say heat rises he says ice they say heat rises he says ice he says ice cold ice heart ice bath. What do you do when you're in pain? Do you ever knock on your rib cage and whisper to your heart. Do you hear it whisper back through the stethoscope? Do you hear it 1 2 3 4.

Caroline Aldridge '21

Hauntings

Danae Younge '20

It had been a full four months since the nightmares had begun seeping through the small cracks in her bedroom windows and had taken control. Cloaked in the moonlit curtains which hung like unanswered questions, the ghosts of her past had tiptoed into her mind and twisted her thoughts and visions. In the middle of the night, death, clothed in military camouflage, would snuggle up beside her while she slept and fill the space her husband used to occupy. There it would be - next to her in the morning when she opened her eyes.

After a month or so, it seemed the ghosts had become accustomed to sunlight because she started seeing them during the day too. They would jump out at her from picture frames and slip into the old suits which hung limp in her closet. Sometimes they would fly off the tongues of news reporters in Afghanistan or simply float by when she stared at the clouds. This was one of those times. As she sat in her office at work, pretending to listen to the ramblings of a coworker on the phone, she looked outside her window in a daze. Wandering thoughts crystallized into a vivid image in front of her - a long outstretched staircase ascending into the the clouds. At the top was her husband, beckoning her, calling out for her to join him and escape the ghosts that haunted her on Earth. And for the first time, she truly considered it.

Sam Grant '19

Emily Holmes '19

For You

Adriana Kim '20

your raincoat never comes off because
you don't ever want to get wet but i think
you really just hate the sun

we breathe in tandem when
your head is in my lap
and you tell me that you wish we were all

little cookie-cutter people
to straighten out your jagged edges
so that you wouldn't bleed
quite so heavily around your borders
but when your eyes are closed I run my hand over the veins on
your neck
I like your rough edges

I don't know if you see me but I see you

your silver spoon became a silver tongue but
you've always hated anything that shines because
your whole life you have been trapped by your silver blood
in that silver home
so
I try not to smile
too much
you never liked a golden girl anyways
or, really
anything at all

sometimes you talk about death when
you are invisible, almost,
hidden by the clouds of smoke you blow from your mouth
because it, you say,
is not a fucking metaphor

because
you like to play with your life, I think,
from every time you climb into my car
bleeding a mix of red and joy
and tell me to drive fast and away
until I don't even know what we're running from
and it scares me
but
I think the pain is how you remind yourself that you're alive

once you told me that you wanted to hurt them back
until you realized
that they wouldn't care if you died —

but I would

I see you

but

I don't know if you see me

so
I shove the death stick between my teeth
wipe the red stains off of my car seats
struggle to support the weight of your broken heart —
it costs me my mind, body, and soul
but
you are my starstuff

you don't want to be saved but,
sweetheart,
you have run too far to give up now
even if the world is an awful, awful place

so
I'll wash my hands in your sadness
polish the crown on your head
let you burn a little black, a little blue,
a little broken, a little fucked up

.

your head is in my lap
and
even when your eyes are closed
you still squint

I cover them with my hands

you really just hate the sun

33

Elli Adams '18

Sam Grant '19

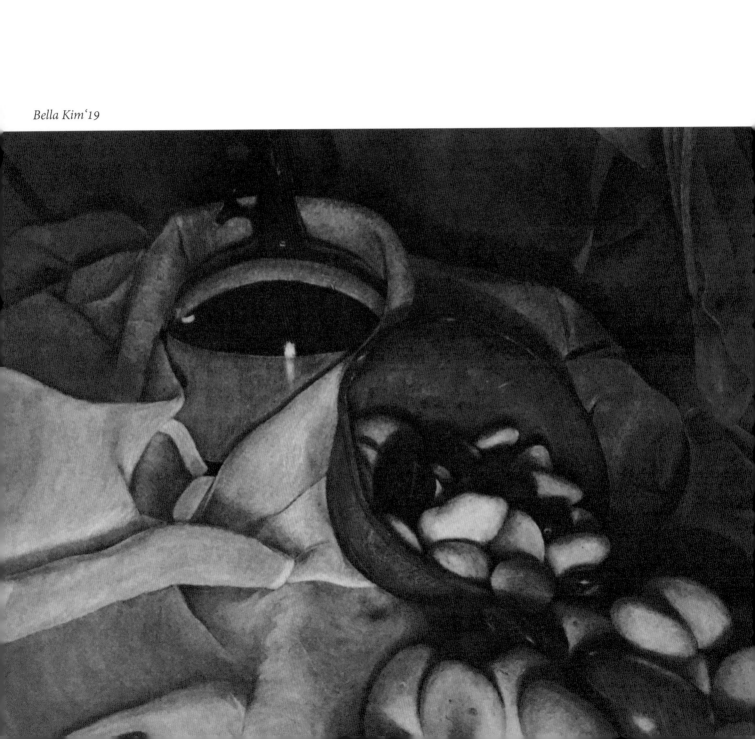

Bella Kim '19

What Was Left

Anonymous

Flat, thin paper.
Her arms, her limbs her heart,
stuck together with glue.
A figure squeezed of meaning,
of dimension,
of everything she used to love.
They meant to paste her
back together,
to bind her to continuous breaths
and the sight of sun in the morning.

Stitched of paper labels
from prescription pills,
they sewed her a skin,
to hide her tears and broken parts.
And crinkled heart.
And with it, they played dress up.

A suit in which she hid behind,
or so they thought.
But they did not realize
that she was no longer hiding;
that she was already gone.
And what was left?
A paper doll.

Alex Hogue '21

The Dream

Ian Layzer '18

They had been sitting in a little row-boat on a river with the afternoon sun kissing their faces. Sarah had been smiling, and her face was so bright and blurry. The whole feeling had the imprecision of a dream of a memory, and Robert never wanted it to end.

Then, a cloud covered the sun, suffocating it. Some crows screamed with cruel joy at this injustice. The sky went black, and the stars were too afraid to come out. Without the sun's warmth, the world began to die, and Robert could see the trees growing by the riverbank wither and perish and crumble into greyness. The crickets went silent. The river choked and slowed to a frozen halt as each water molecule faltered and then failed, slumping into an ugly latticework of ice.

An immense feeling of guilt consumed Robert, and it was as if it had been his fault that the cloud had murdered the sun and that the world was ending. He felt very cold, saw that Sarah had disappeared, and then felt alone as well. The row-boat cracked and groaned, and he felt himself pitch backwards, falling through the ice and into darkness. As he fell, he heard her scream all around him.

It was with a sense of abrupt finality that Robert awoke from his wife, and he knew that that was the last time he would see her. The despair of the broken scene from which he had just escaped was beginning to wear off, though his room was cold and hard and hardly welcoming. He got out of bed and walked over to the sink, where he washed his face and combed his scraggly hair into a respectable order. For a moment, he wished for a mirror but then realized that he did not want to see his gaunt face because it would just incite him to anger and hatred.

An hour later, Robert was eating breakfast. He looked over and saw Joe standing in the corner, carefully sipping his coffee to avoid spilling any on his pressed uniform. Today's meal was special because Robert had gotten to choose the food, and the chef had agreed to make anything as long as the total expenditure did not exceed twenty dollars. This had left Robert with some important arithmetic to determine the maximum amount of food he could ask for because if he was anything it was economical. The result was one bagel and cream cheese, two fried eggs, four strips of bacon, a hunk of ham, and a cup of mediocre coffee. The different fats and oils melted into a melancholic symphony in his mouth, though he had to fight his mind to keep it all from turning to ash and ignore the sinking feeling he'd been unable to shake since his dream.

At eleven, after he had finished eating and had cleaned up, Robert went to see Father Brown, and Joe walked with him, though they didn't speak to each other. Father Brown was a kindly clean-shaven man, and his office was the only place Robert felt comfortable and forgiven. Robert sat down and looked into Father Brown's eyes, occasionally glancing at the depiction of Christ's crucifixion that was hanging on the wall. He had regretfully neglected Jesus for most of his life but in the past few months had started coming to services again. He wanted God's comfort and love and to be safe from torment. They danced around the only subject that mattered, even though it seemed that now was the time to talk about it. Mostly they talked about the Lord and His love and His forgiveness.

For a moment, Robert doubted again. The cold doubt spread through him like a disease, corrupting the warmth of his faith. He felt a sick fear of the dark future and started crying. It was only by holding Father Brown's wrinkled hand for a while and focusing on his smile that he was able fight back and reinstate in himself what was so necessary at that moment. God loved him and would welcome him into His kingdom.

Joe knocked and entered and said that their time was up. He wasn't smiling. Robert wanted to protest that it wasn't time yet, that they hadn't waited long enough, but he didn't. He and Father Brown stood up from their seats and walked out with Joe. The walk through the building went too fast, though Robert tried to savor every step of it, to slow their pace as much as possible. He moved his head around as they walked, trying to soak in every detail and every solemn face that stared at him.

When they finally exited the maze of brick and metal into the daylight, Robert was blinded. The noon sun high above him was not gentle or comforting but harsh and accusatory. It knew about the dream and what Robert had done and wanted to punish him for it. Robert hung his head in pain and shame as they continued to walk through the yard and then up some wood stairs onto a platform.

Standing there, he looked around and saw a horde of unsmiling people collected in the courtyard, watching him. All of their faces and their silence seemed to jump out and scream at him. Father Brown rested his hand on Robert's back and Robert calmed down a little. Suddenly, a thick cloth hood was pulled over his face, and for the second time that day, he was thrown into darkness. He felt a coarse rope pressed against and around his neck, squeezing God out of him. Father Brown's hand was gone, and Robert was alone and afraid. He wasn't thinking about Sarah's forgiveness anymore, just his own fear. Then, the floor was gone and he felt himself falling and falling further into the darkness. There was no bright flash of glorious light, just cold darkness.

Sam Grant '19

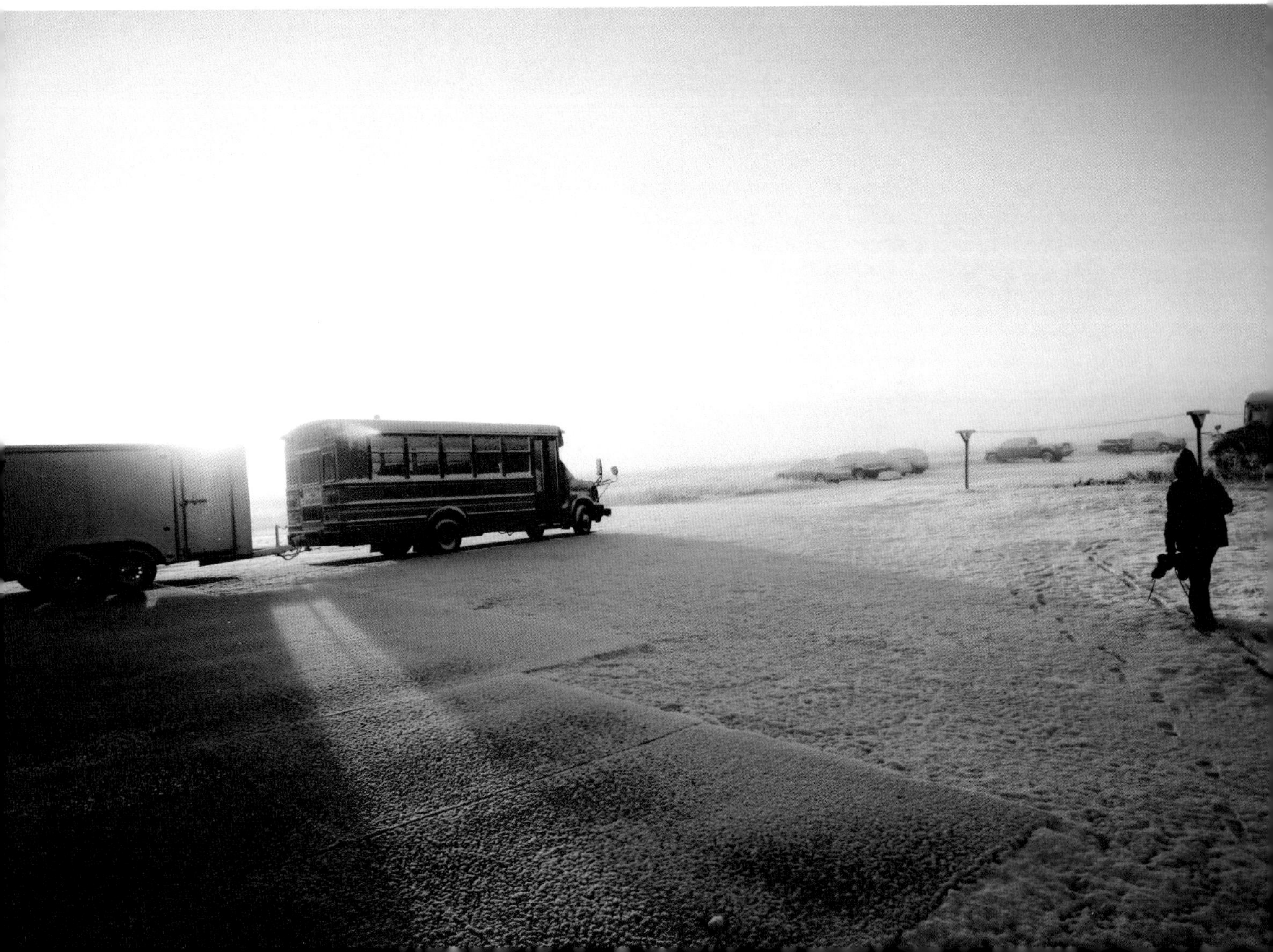

Sam Grant '19

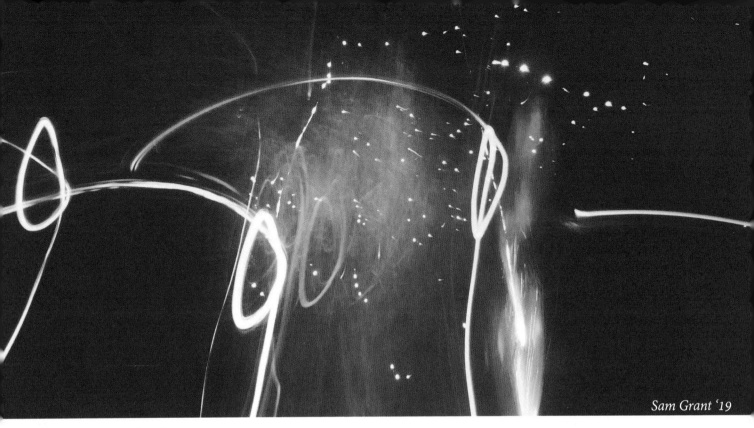

On writing

Ian Layzer '18

My hand is shackled to the font of you,
which spews forth lyric blood through inky veins.
Prometheus, I mold clay names in chains,
as every line is created anew.
I wrestle with your adolescent coup;
an uprising against your maker strains
to burst the metric prison that remains
and let poetic beauty shine all through.
Then finally, you break away and fly—
I can't control your dauntless dream and zeal
to shirk the petty confines of design.
And everyone that reads your call so high,
whose hearts do grasp your passionate appeal,
will be forever changed by one stray line.

Sam Grant '19

III.
how we live

Dollar Pier Closed

Lillia Larson '18

I place fifteen quarters on a door-frame
To ease my conscience. "All in, now!" my spirit spits
at us three gambling goblins. Check, check, check;
Wood wedging into fingernails like claws. We the same?
Guilty pleasures to make a deal, a pact, a virtue with it
Like Faust at night. Just soak in the unadulterated ocean—
Water closing in like the bubonic plague. All alone there swelling
Like brain-eating amoebas. Still as a whisker; sharp as a whisper.
A red-eyed lens turns to us, smiling. A cannon-ball of lights flashing like
Finger-licking cannibals: Lunging to catch, snatch, our feet snap
And unlatch. "Jump the fence!" it screams — "Look at the
mangling trapeze off the edge," shriek my ulcerations.
The king waves are flushing, untying our knots;
Wind ceases over the unwieldy wooden fence.
Dismembered rattails streak blood
across the pier and back.

Guilt is the mouthpiece of the conscience. Take a blow and learn from it.

Virginia Capehart '18

Empty But One

Lillia Larson '18

There's a chorus of sorrys
into which I want to join
but I don't like the spotlight
and joining in now would break the score
And I'll tell you improvisation never ends well in my chorus.
      The chorus of sorrys is supposed to be ended with my voice. My scratchy voice more than likely accompanied with a hiccup.
That last syllable stuck in my throat.
I've got stage fright
and I don't think I can play my role.
I've never sung well in this chorus
I don't remember my lines… Well I do remember my lines I've been saying them under my breath
forever until my throat gets scratchy and I need a drink of water,
but I forget them every time I get a cue.
I choke and turn and I flee from backstage,
leaving the
                        empty-but-one
theatre unaware of my previous presence
or else aware but knowing I would not be participating that day
but maybe tomorrow.
      Applause is seductive
      but unlikely with my unpreparedness to be in the chorus.
The more likely ending is one of an awkward finish to the beautiful sorrys which leaves the
                      empty-but-one
theatre with an uncomfortable feeling
      Where you can't appropriately divert your eyes but desperately want to
      as the embarrassment of the actor radiates strongly,
           so strongly that you feel the mood rotting and a gross,
                icky feeling wrenches at your heart
                    and tells you to run from the padded seats
                        and separate yourself from it,
                            Run, run away until the icky feeling
                            stops chasing you
                              and leaves you
                                  to our own regrets.

Sam Grant ‘19

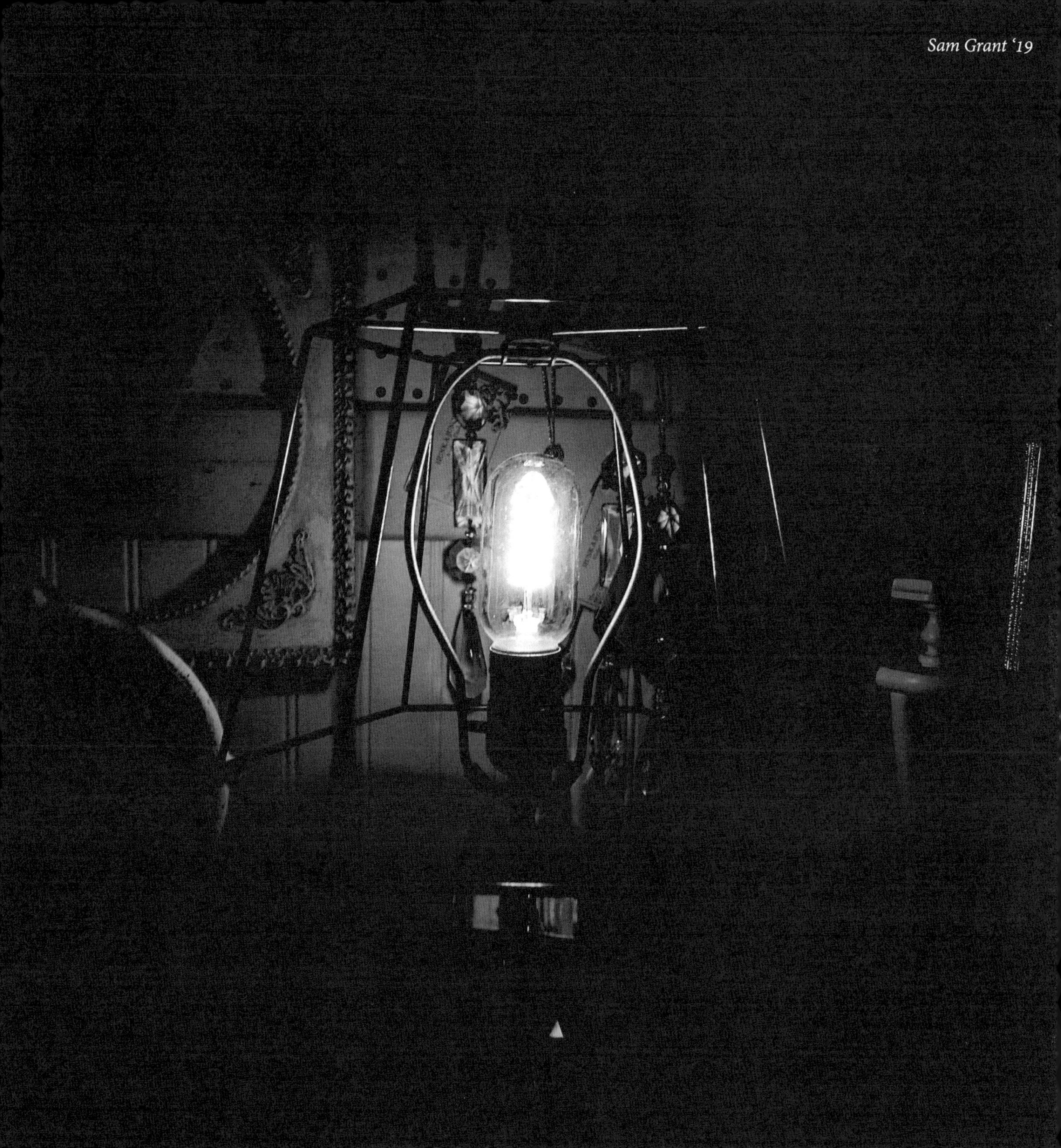

Sam Grant '19

Time Passes

Austen Dellinger '18

young,
and no longer
afraid.
she finds herself
in this house
stationed
between the open field and the sea and the sky,
turned gray.
her auburn hair,
sometime, without her even noticing,
unraveled.
all her plans
play out in her mind, and she wonders when
she can begin. all her days
await her, and there is nothing left
in her way. endings
unknown to her. she is quiet.
the world is still.

she sits on her stoop: beautiful, stoic too. thin
streams of wind brush against her as
the evening wanes--
too much of it has passed. already
life beckons, but
the walls are still unfinished.

she has, left before her,
all the time
she needs.

                     Time passes.

she needs
all the time
she has left before her.

the walls are still. unfinished
life beckons, but
too much of it has passed, already.
the evening wanes.
streams of wind brush against her as
she sits on her stoop: beautiful, stoic, too thin.

the world is still
unknown to her. she is quiet,
in her way. endings
await her, and there is nothing left
she can begin. all her days
play out in her mind, and she wonders when
all her plans
unraveled.
sometime, without her even noticing,
her auburn hair
turned gray,
between the open field and the sea and the sky.
stationed
in this house,
she finds herself
afraid,
and no longer
Young.

Hero

Colby Preston '21

She was seated on a humongous white bat. It was a corpse, recently-dead, one of her spoils of war. I watched, from the crowd. She was happy. Of course she was, she was the hero. Heroes are happy. They would fight some terror, protect the city for a couple more years, and then get killed by their own ego. My favourite was a young girl a teenager, really two heroes ago who I thought was going to survive her own hubris. I still remember her, she had caramel skin, the kind from movies, flawless.
That girl died.
There aren't any more movies.
I bet this hero will too. She seems alright, now, but I can see the glint in her eyes as she laughs, the pretentiousness behind her supposed humility. I think I hate her. I think I hate heroes. If they could just understand that it has to be them who refuses to continue the cycle, and not the next poor battle-weary soul, I might not hate them.
But they don't.
They don't open their eyes.
The sky is gray. It has been for a while.
The people aren't gray, they wear clothes dyed in all sorts of silly colors. Never white, though. White is the color of the things the heroes kill. The things the heroes become when they get too pompous. The heroes don't think they become those things, but they do. I think I'm too young to hate people. I still think I hate heroes.
I was right, I was right, I'm always right. This latest hero, the one who killed the bat, only lasted two years before she mysteriously disappeared she didn't disappear and a large white lioness started stalking the city she's the lioness, this is so obvious. The one who killed the lioness was a skinny Asian boy. He looked surprised during the parades, like he didn't really get why he was there. He thinks he's in touch with his roots now, but give him a taste of the high life and he doesn't stop. None of them do.
My favourite disappeared, and then a crow the size of a parking complex terrorized the city. Sometimes I wonder what sort of thing people would fight if I was a hero, and disappeared. I sometimes wonder whether I should fight one of the things that come once the heroes disappear, just once, to see if I could stop the… decay.
But that's the thinking of heroes.
And I'm not a hero.

Lauren Harpole '18

Grace Gordan '19

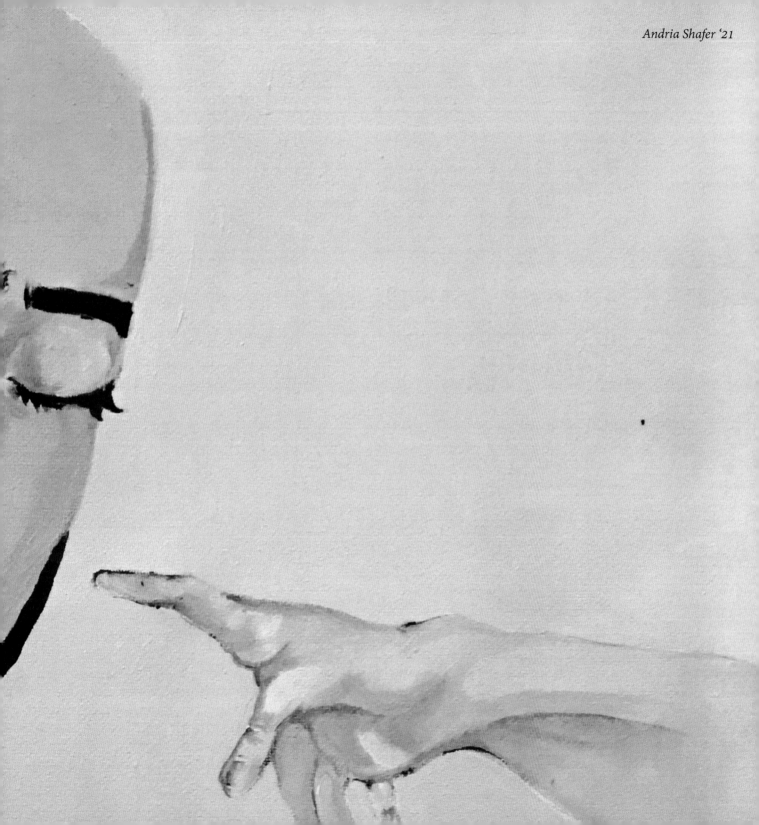

Andria Shafer '21

Anna West '19

Timeless Memories

Isabella Strauss '20

Timeless Memories
She traveled the world to always stay young.
Her sense of adventure was contagious.
Thrilling stories from the tip of her tongue,
Her soothing voice, I hope never changes.

Her ocean blue eyes look deep into mine.
Her healing arms wrapped around me at night.
Assuring me everything will be fine,
The ones she loved, she held so very tight.

But do her stories matter anymore,
When her memory starts to fade away?
What happened to the Grandma I adore?
Her laughs and smiles are missed each passing day.

Now constant chatter turns into silence,
But to me, memories remain timeless.

How to Speak

Anonymous

Today, I plan to teach myself how to speak.
My mother taught me the words
My father, their meanings
Now I must take them
The words, and their meanings
And make them fit my own bleeding truth
I must strip them of their suits
And dress them in my boots
Then maybe I can take them out some night
And not feel pressured to be something
For that light across the room
That offers me a drink
And kindly pours it down my throat
Then asks me how I'm doing
Like he's something I'm pursuing
How wooing.
Maybe I can take words and their meanings to a gathering
And not have to assume
That his blathering about my sweater
Is permission to take it off
And my cough of course means yes.
But I have to confess that maybe I did say yes
And maybe he did better
Maybe he really liked my sweater
I guess words and their meanings are the only ones
Who'd let her. Remember.
The Tula-dan-dasana

not like a broken umbrella
like a capital T
Truth is that silence breeds silence
But what if the violence of my own thoughts
Is what I sought
What if the depths of my sorrow
Help me forget about tomorrow
And let me borrow
A piece of individuality
The reality is that
Sexuality is the only real mentality
And although we are tethered
It's okay because love lasts forever
So the words and their meanings don't matter.
Right?

editors-in-chief

Olivia Chilkoti
Austen Dellinger
Sean Rutledge

staff

Spencer Adler
Caroline Aldridge
Maggie Chambliss
Octavia Chilkoti
Morgan Doyle
Grace Gordon
Lily Gordon
Alex Hogue
Sarah Kim
Elizabeth Kohn
Ian Layzer
Mira Pickus
Eleanor Robb
Carina Rockart
Andria Shafer
Danae Younge

faculty advisor

Dr. Lauren Garrett, English

acknowledgments

We've had a wonderful time creating *Exurbia* this year, and so many people contributed to the making of this journal. First, thank you to **Dr. Lauren Garrett**, who amidst teaching and having a baby managed to keep us on track. An additional thank you to **Dr. Abby Seeskin** for the continued use of her room in Dr. Garrett's absence. Next, we would like to thank the **Exurbia staff** for their thoughtful comments and suggestions for submissions throughout the year. And finally, thank you to all the **Durham Academy students and faculty** represented in the 2017-2018 edition of *Exurbia* who not only choose to express themselves through their words and art, but who are also willing to share that expression with us and with the wider community.

Made in the USA
Columbia, SC
06 May 2018